PEOPLE & PLACES

U.S.S.R.

Written by
Ludmilla Lewis and Marilyn Tolhurst

Consultant Ludmilla Lewis

Illustrated by
Ann Savage

MACMILLAN

A TEMPLAR BOOK

First published in Great Britain in 1988
by Macmillan Children's Books
A division of Macmillan Publishers Ltd
4 Little Essex Street
London WC2R 3LF and Basingstoke

Devised and produced by Templar Publishing Ltd
107 High Street, Dorking, Surrey RH4 1QA

Copyright © 1988 by Templar Publishing Ltd
Illustrations copyright © 1988 by Templar Publishing Ltd

All rights reserved. No part of this publication may be reproduced, stored in a retrieval system, or transmitted by any means, electronic, mechanical, photocopying, recording or otherwise, without the prior permission of the publishers or copyright holders.

Editor Steve Parker
Designers Patrick Nugent, Bridget Morley
Photo-researcher Hugh Olliff
Studio services Kenneth Ward

Colour separations by Positive Colour Ltd, Maldon, Essex
Printed by L.E.G.O., Vicenza, Italy

British Library Cataloguing in Publication Data
Lewis, Ludmilla
  USSR.–(People & Places).–(A Templar book).
  1. Russia–Juvenile literature
  I. Title   II. Tolhurst, Marilyn   III. Series
  947.085'4   DK18

ISBN 0 333 45715 3

Contents

One-Seventh of the World	6
The Mother Tongue	8
Land of Contrasts	10
The Last Great Wilderness	12
Across the USSR	14
Nature's Riches	16
The World of Work	18
Uniting the Republics	20
Lands of the Tsar	22
Revolution!	24
The Union at War	26
Comrades in Communism	28
Religion and the State	30
Art and Architecture	32
Masters in Words and Music	34
School Days	36
Looking After the People	38
Vanya's Day	40
Cabbage Soup and Vodka	42
The Soviet Union and the Future	44
Index	46

ONE-SEVENTH OF THE WORLD

The USSR is the biggest country in the world. It stretches across two continents, Europe and Asia. It is about two and a half times the size of the USA and 90 times bigger than Britain. Because of its vastness it contains every kind of scenery imaginable, from deserts to mountains, forests to grassy plains, to the frozen northern wastes of Siberia.

The USSR is often wrongly called "Russia". In fact Russia is one of the 15 separate republics or regions which make up the Union of Soviet Socialist Republics (USSR), sometimes known as the Soviet Union. Moscow is the capital of both the republic of Russia and the whole of the USSR, and it is the centre of government, the arts and business.

The USSR is governed by the Communist Party. This means that land and industries are controlled not by individual people or families but by the state (see page 28). Because of this communist style of government, as well as its vast size and military strength, the USSR is mistrusted by many Western countries. This has caused a barrier to the understanding of ordinary Soviet people.

Symbols of the USSR

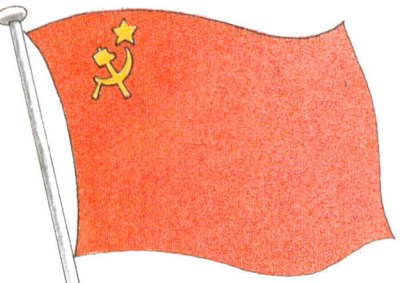

The Soviet flag is red, the colour of socialism and revolution. The yellow hammer and sickle represent the union of industry and agriculture.

The huge Red Square, containing the beautiful St Basil's Cathedral, lies in the centre of Moscow. Soviet military parades are held there each May Day, the traditional socialist celebration date.

Moscow
The capital and largest city in the USSR. It has a population of nearly nine million people and is a centre for industry.

Leningrad
Formerly called St Petersburg, after its founder Peter the Great. This city was the scene of the 1917 revolution.

Statue of Peter the Great, Leningrad

Estonian ice-breaker

KEY FACTS

▶ The USSR is a union of 15 republics, of which Russia is one of the largest.
▶ The population is about 250 million.
▶ Moscow is the nation's capital and largest city, and also the capital of the republic of Russia.
▶ The nearest and most important neighbours are Poland, China and Japan. There are nine other countries bordering the USSR, as well as two oceans and several seas.
▶ The unit of money is the *rouble*, which is divided into 100 *kopeks*.
▶ The USSR has a land area of 21,274,200 square kilometres.

Key
- Lowlands
- Uplands
- Mountains
- Alpine Mountains

Tallin
This city is the capital of Estonia and an important port on the often ice-bound Baltic Coast. Ice-breakers are used to keep the shipping lanes open.

Kiev
Kiev is the capital of the Ukraine, a major wheat-growing area. The city was rebuilt after massive destruction in World War 2.

7

THE MOTHER TONGUE

The official language of the USSR is Russian. It is taught everywhere and is the main means of communication across the nation. It is, however, only one of about 160 languages spoken by the various peoples in the country.

Some Soviet children may have to learn three languages at school: official Russian, the language of their republic, and their own national or tribal language. Some of the southern areas of the USSR have a language similar to Arabic, while mountain regions often have several different dialects within a small area.

Russian, like English, comes from the Indo-European language spoken thousands of years ago. The Russian alphabet is different from ours and may look odd at first. It is called "Cyrillic" after St Cyril, a Greek missionary who taught the religion of Christianity to the Russians in the 9th century. He invented his own alphabet, taking some letters from Greek and some from Latin. The modern Russian alphabet of 32 letters is based on this.

Here is the news...
The official Soviet news agency is TASS. It provides news about the USSR for radio and TV stations and newspapers around the world. All its news is controlled by the government.

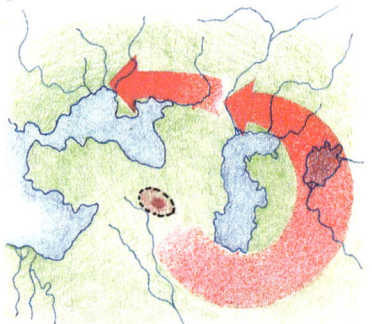

The Indo-European language
Of the 19 most common languages in the modern world, 11 have come from the ancient Indo-European language. The dotted line shows the area between the Black Sea and the Caspian Sea, where this language came from. The arrows show how it spread.

А a	Б b	В v	Г g	Д d	Е ye
father	bat	vat	get	dog	yet

Л l	М m	Н n	О o	П p	Р r
long	map	name	dot	pet	ran

Ч ch	Ш sh	Щ shch	Ъ -	Ы i	Ь -
chat	ship	push-chair	(silent)	pit	(silent)

WORKERS OF THE WORLD UNITE!
Communist Party of the Soviet Union

ПРАВДА

Paper founded on 5 May 1912 by V. I. LENIN

Publication of the Central Committee of the CPSU

No 138 (247607) • Sunday 18 May 1986 Issue No 1 • Price 50p

Part of the front page of *Pravda's* English language edition

Telling the truth?
Pravda is the main Russian newspaper. The name means "Truth", although it may not tell the whole truth. Many people from the West think that *Pravda* prints only what the government wants the people to know.

Signs in the street
To Western eyes, some Russian words look like English written backwards! Russian is a relatively easy language for foreign people to learn and write, but it may be difficult for them to pronounce the sounds properly.

Ё yo	Ж zh	З z	И ee	Й y	К k
yonder	vision	zebra	meet	yellow	king
С s	Т t	У oo	Ф f	Х ch	Ц ts
sing	top	soon	fat	loch	pets
Э eh	Ю yoo	Я ar			
any	few	ya			

The Russian alphabet
Here is a simple pronunciation guide to the Russian alphabet. It shows each letter's equivalent sound in English, and gives an English word containing that sound.

9

LAND OF CONTRASTS

A citizen of Leningrad, in the west of the USSR, arrives at work at nine o'clock in the morning. At the same moment a person in Anadyr, on the east coast, relaxes at home – it is seven o'clock in the evening. This gives some idea of the vastness of the Soviet Union, which wraps itself almost halfway round the globe and covers 11 time zones.

The weather varies dramatically across the country. Siberia, in the north, is the coldest inhabited place on earth. The Karakum desert, in the south, is one of the hottest and driest areas in the world.

Much of the central Soviet Union lies in northerly latitudes, far from the sea. Like the mid-west of the USA, it has what's called a continental climate, with very cold winters and hot summers. Spring comes suddenly in April, often accompanied by floods as ice and snow quickly melt. All farming work is crowded into the short summer season, before winter grips the land again. In contrast, the warm sub-tropical area near the Black Sea, in the south, is a busy holiday resort.

A citizen from Siberia, dressed in traditionally-patterned fur clothing and snow goggles.

Siberia
In this most northerly part of the Soviet Union, the ground is frozen solid for most of the year. In the Omyakon Valley temperatures fall to –65°C! Soft fur-and-skin boots, a sheepskin coat and a fur hat are a must against the bone-chilling cold. Below –50°C all outdoor work stops. The summer lasts for only one month but is quite warm.

Georgia

The republic of Georgia, near the Black Sea, has a sub-tropical climate like Florida or the South of France. There are sandy beaches, palm trees and an average of 200 sunny days each year.

The Karakum desert

In this desert in Turkmenia, summer temperatures reach 50°C and no rain falls for months on end. Blazing daytime heat quickly gives way to chilly nights, and strong winds shift the sands constantly. The desert-dwellers wear loose canvas robes and shoes, with fur hats for protection against the fierce sun. All work stops during the hottest part of the day.

THE LAST GREAT WILDERNESS

In the Soviet Union there are four main kinds of countryside: tundra, taiga, steppe, and desert.
The tundra is in the north, inside the Arctic Circle. Winter lasts for nine months, the ground is frozen and cold winds sweep over the snow. Yet even in this icy wilderness reindeer, polar bears, Arctic foxes and many other animals are able to survive.

The taiga is an enormous central area of coniferous forests, with pine and fir trees stretching unbroken for hundreds of kilometres. It teems with wildlife including brown bears, lynxes and wolves. The great rivers and lakes of the taiga include the River Ob, the longest in the USSR, and the gigantic Lake Baikal, which contains many strange fish that are found nowhere else.

The steppe is a region of sparse woodland which gradually thins out and gives way to endless areas of grassy plain. Once the land of the Cossack horseman, the steppe is now the main grain-growing area of the Soviet Union.

The deserts have little plant life, but even so lizards, snakes and camels manage to survive there.

Hero and villain
The wolf has disappeared in most parts of Europe but it is still common deep in the forests of the USSR. It plays a major part in Soviet folktales – in some stories it is a villain, in others it is the hero.

Beluga (Russian sturgeon)

The finest food
Russian black caviar is one of the world's most expensive foods. It is the salted roe, or eggs, of the female sturgeon.

This strange-looking, armour-plated fish is a slow swimmer and feeds on worms and shellfish. It can grow to over 3 metres in length.

Black caviar

KEY FACTS

▶ The River Ob is the longest in the USSR, at 5,570 kilometres.
▶ Lake Baikal is the deepest lake in the world. In some places it goes down 1,620 metres.
▶ More than 350 rivers flow into Lake Baikal, but only one flows out – the Angara.
▶ More than three-quarters of the fish in Lake Baikal occur nowhere else in the world.
▶ Fishing is a major sport in the Soviet Union. One person in 11 is a keen angler.

Beautiful fur coat
Snow leopards are extremely rare. They inhabit remote mountain regions and in the past they were hunted for their beautiful, thick, warm fur. They eat deer, wild sheep and boars, as well as small creatures such as hares, marmots and birds.

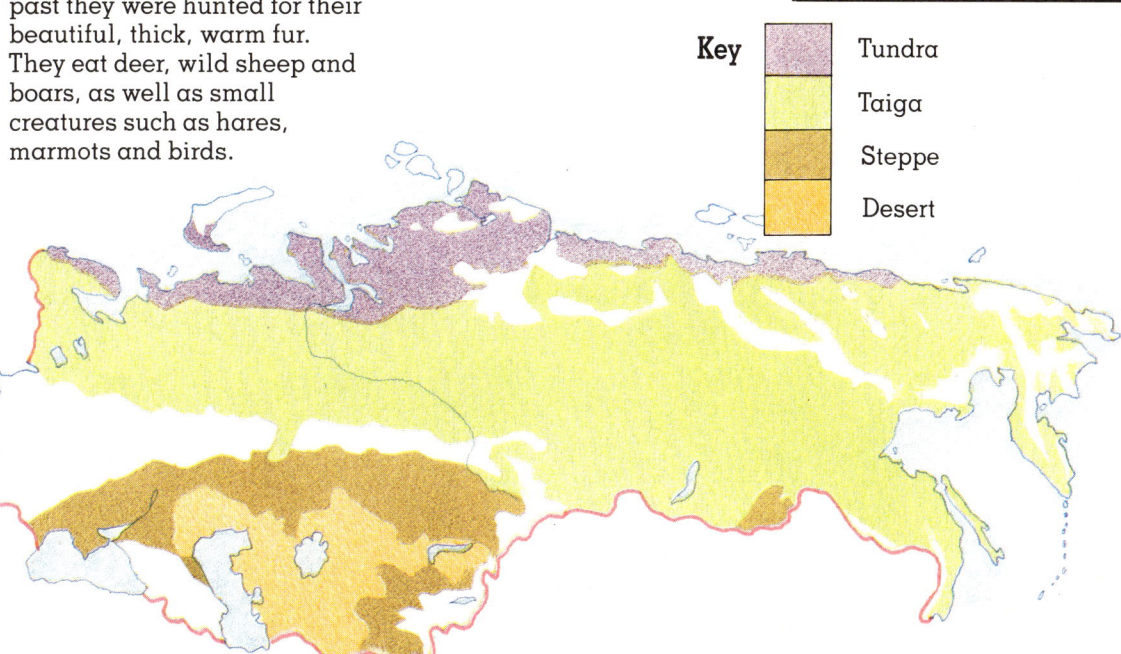

Key
- Tundra
- Taiga
- Steppe
- Desert

The wild lands
The map shows the main types of landscape in the USSR. The white areas are mostly mountains, farmlands or built-up areas. The conifer forests of the taiga stretch unbroken for hundreds of kilometres. They are among the largest natural areas left on earth. Some very rare animals live in the forest reserves, such as European bison and wild boars. They have died out in many other places.

ACROSS THE USSR

Travelling around the Soviet Union has always been difficult. Much of the country is mountainous, frozen or flooded, or suffers from sandstorms or earthquakes. In the past, people used various pack animals, including reindeer, horses, donkeys and camels, according to the region and climate.

Waterways have always been important transport routes. Even today, rivers such as the Volga carry many ships and barges. Ice-breakers keep the ports and rivers open in the cold northerly areas.

The first railways were built in the European part of Russia. Then in the 1890s tracks were built, crossing the tundra and desert to the farthest parts of the country. The Trans-Siberian Railway is the world's longest continuous railway line.

Despite massive road-building programmes during this century, parts of the USSR can still not be reached by road. Airstrips are now common in places that have few cars and that have never seen a train. Small aircraft are a major means of transport. Aeroflot, the Soviet airline, carries more passengers each year than any other airline in the world.

The "impossible road"
The Chuya Highway crosses the Altai Mountains of the southern USSR. It is 626 kilometres long and was built in the 1930s to transport the great mineral wealth from the region. The builders had to hack their way through rocks, tunnel through hillsides and suspend bridges over mountain gorges.

Winter travel
The *troika*, a three-horse sleigh, is a traditional way of travelling in winter. Today it is used more for fun. In the city parks these sleighs are a popular tourist attraction.

Underground palaces
The Moscow Metro underground railway, built in the 1930s, is famous for its beauty and cleanliness. Many of the 100 or so stations were built of marble and decorated with chandeliers and paintings. A ticket costs five *kopecks* (about five pence) for any length of journey.

The world's longest railway
The Trans-Siberian Railway runs across the nation from Leningrad to Nakhodka. It is about 9,500 kilometres long and the full journey takes eight days.

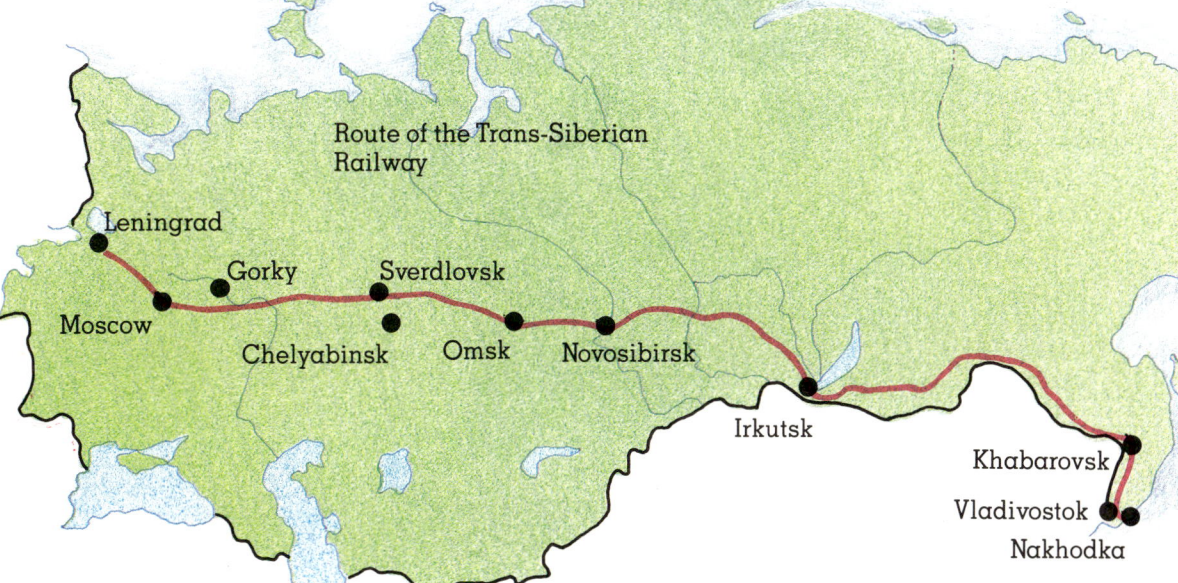

NATURE'S RICHES

One-quarter of the world's forests are found in the USSR and the timber industry is an important part of the country's economy. Trees are cut down to make wood products of all kinds, including furniture, pencils, toys and matches. (Look at a box of matches. It may well be "Made in the USSR".) The great rivers of the taiga are used to transport the cut logs, either by ship or by floating them along in great rafts.

The steppe lands are the main areas for crop-growing. The "Black Earth" region of the Ukraine is especially fertile and produces enormous quantities of wheat, rye, sugarbeet and potatoes.

Farther south, in Armenia and Georgia, the warm climate supports tea plantations, vineyards and orchards, as well as the "white gold" of the southern regions – cotton.

The Soviet Union also has plentiful supplies of minerals, including coal, iron, oil, gas, gold, silver and precious gems. Siberia is particularly rich in minerals. Much effort has been put into building roads, railways and towns in the region, so that the minerals can be mined and transported to factories in the west of the country.

Dolls inside dolls
These traditional "Russian doll" toys are one of the many wood products for which the Soviet Union is famous.

Farming in the Ukraine

The farms of the USSR are not privately owned by one person or family. They are collective farms known as *kolkhoz*. Here a farm worker in the Kazakhstan region has won an award for high grain yields – a specially baked loaf!

Siberian gems

The name Siberia comes from the Tartar words *Sib ir*, meaning "sleeping land". Today the land is no longer sleeping. Engineers and miners are moving in to obtain oil, rare metals and gemstones like the ones shown here. The USSR has the world's largest reserves of coal, natural gas, iron ore, chrome and magnesium.

Moonstone
Gold
Star ruby
Ruby
Lapis lazuli
Turquoise
Amethyst
Topaz
Jade

17

THE WORLD OF WORK

The Soviet Union has some of the largest mineral resources in the world. It produces almost every kind of mineral and metal, from coal and oil to diamonds and gold. Hydro-electric power, made by damming the great rivers, provides one-quarter of the energy used by the country. Nuclear power stations have also been built. However, the disaster at Chernobyl in 1986 (the worst nuclear accident in the world) has made people even more cautious about nuclear power.

Many Soviet workers are employed in engineering. The great factories produce mostly industrial machinery, tractors and heavy vehicles. Videos, hi-fis, private cars and some other consumer goods are still fairly rare.

Collective farms known as *kolkhoz* produce much of the nation's food. The land and machinery are owned by groups of people, not individuals. The workers are paid according to their output. There are also state collective farms called *sovkhoz* which are run like factories, often specializing in one type of food.

KEY FACTS

▶ In the USSR most power comes from coal, oil, natural gas and hydro-electricity.
▶ Siberia produces one-quarter of the USSR's electricity output.
▶ Siberia also accounts for one-third of the USSR's timber industry, and it rivals South Africa in the production of gold and diamonds.
▶ The fur industry is important in the forest regions. Sable (a stoat-like animal), fox and squirrel pelts are very costly. Many of the fur garments worn by ordinary people come from animals bred on "fur farms".
▶ All industry is owned by the state.

Lada cars
The brand-new town of Togliatti, on the River Volga, is the site of a new Lada factory. The Lada organization produces vehicles in co-operation with the Italian company Fiat. Here car bodies are carried to the next part of the assembly line.

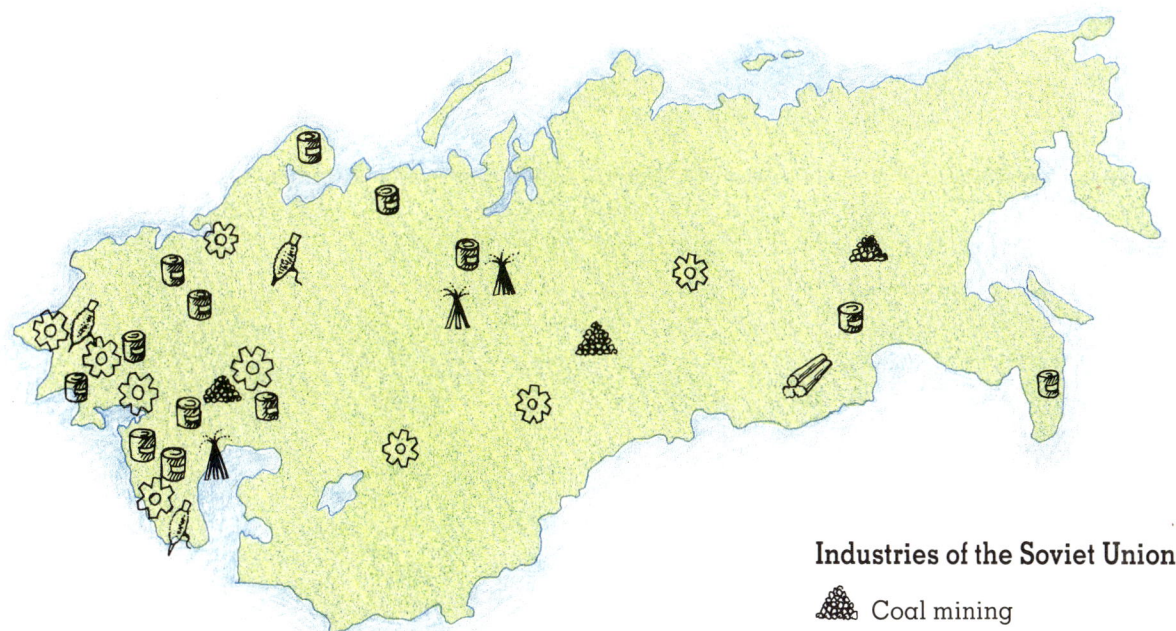

Industries of the Soviet Union

- Coal mining
- Food and drink processing
- Timber, wood pulp and paper
- Machinery and engineering
- Light industries
- Oil and petrochemicals

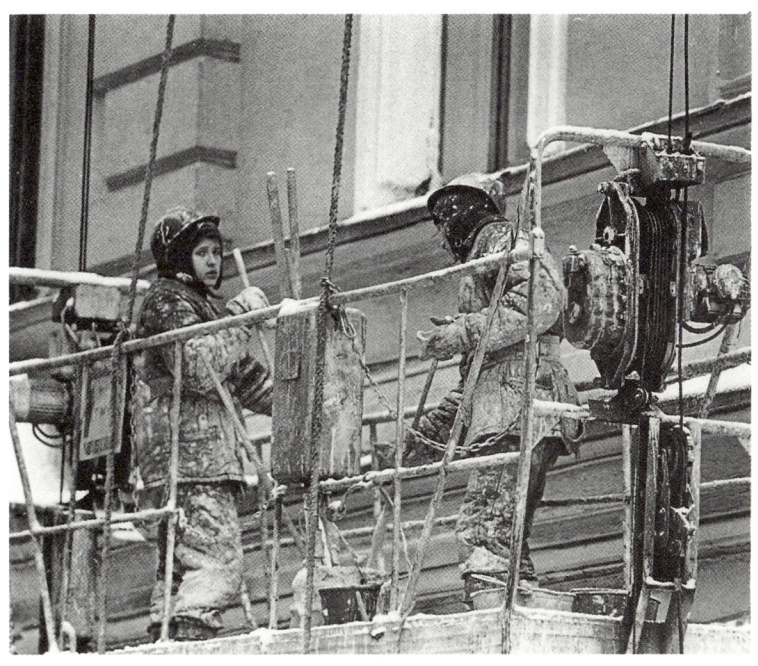

Working women

There is virtually no unemployment in the USSR. Four out of five Soviet women have jobs. They often do heavy work which in other countries is usually done by men – for example, mining, building and engineering. Some factories provide nurseries or creches for the young children. These women are painting an office building in Moscow's bitter winter weather.

UNITING THE REPUBLICS

Within the 15 republics that make up the USSR there are people of more than 100 nationalities, ranging from the fair-haired and blue-eyed people of the Baltic region to the dark-haired and round-faced Yakuts of Siberia. Each group has its own customs and culture. The Russians themselves, who belong to a broad group called the Slavs, make up over half the population. They are famous for their folk customs and colourful national dress.

The Asiatic part of the USSR is an area of many different tribes, such as the Uzbeks, Turkmens, Kazakhs and Tartars. They are mostly of Turkish or Mongolian origin. Another Asiatic tribe, the Turkics, are excellent horse-riders and weave beautiful carpets.

During this century great efforts have been made to unite the different groups under one leadership. More than 1,000 new towns have been built since 1917, and new roads and railways link areas that were previously cut-off. Even so, there are still great differences in lifestyle across the country. On the windy plains of central Asia, wandering shepherd families live almost side by side with modern flat-dwellers in newly-built towns.

Byelorussian folk dancer

Song and dance
Woven fabrics, bright colours and intricate embroidery are features of the traditional Russian costumes. Folk dance groups are popular both at home and abroad, with their joyous music and acrobatic dancing.

Regional costumes

Here are some of the traditional costumes worn in different regions of the USSR. The dancer on the left comes from the Byelorussian republic, in the west of the country, around Minsk.

Uzbek "skullcaps" worn by women

Uzbek headgear

Georgian costumes

Tazikstan headgear

Old and new

Samarkand is one of the legendary cities of central Asia. It is more than 2,500 years old, and was capital of the fabulous Mongolian empire of Timur during the 14th century. The front entrance and the domes of the Shah-i-Zindah group of mausoleums (large and stately tombs) are shown here.

LANDS OF THE TSAR

The word *tsar* means "emperor". For 300 years between 1613 and 1917, tsars of the Romanov family ruled Russia. They had complete power over the country and people, they chose their own governments and they waged their own wars.

One of the most famous tsars was Peter the Great, who ruled from 1682 to 1725. He founded the city of St Petersburg and extended Russia's territories by victories over the Turks and Swedes. Catherine the Great, who was empress of Russia from 1762 to 1796, continued her country's expansion and conquered parts of Turkey and Poland.

Ordinary people were poor and their food was simple and scarce, mostly black bread and cabbage. The poorest of all, the *moujiks* (serfs), belonged to the local landowner or the tsar, and they could be bought and sold with the land.

By the beginning of this century Russia was a vast but somewhat backward nation. While other countries in Europe were becoming more democratic, with governments elected by the people, Russia was still under the control of the tsar.

Absolute power
The tsars had complete rule over their country:
▶ The tsar controlled all the lands and people in Russia. This system of rule is called autocracy, with absolute power concentrated in the hands of one person.
▶ Romanov was the surname of the Russian royal family, who ruled from 1613 to the revolution of 1917.
▶ Many of the serfs who built St Petersburg (now Leningrad) died during the work. Their bodies are buried in the foundations of the city.
▶ Serfs in Russia had little more freedom than farm animals, being the property of landowners. In 1861 Tsar Alexander II freed them so that they could buy their own land.

Ivan the Terrible
Ivan IV was the first official Russian tsar. He ruled from 1547 to 1584 (at about the time of England's Elizabeth I). He was known as Ivan the Terrible because of his temper and cruelty. He killed his eldest son in a fit of rage, and he had the architect of St Basil's Cathedral blinded so that he could never again build anything of such beauty.

Hard times on the land

Under the tsars, Russian peasants had tough lives. Their villages of log cabins were scattered among woods and fields. They farmed the land during the summer and spent the long winters at home, making lace, wooden toys or perhaps harmonicas, according to the speciality of the region. They were often deeply religious and had strong local customs which stayed unchanged over generations.

Emperor at the age of 10

Peter the Great began his rule at the age of 10. He was the first tsar to travel outside Russia, and once he worked as a ship's carpenter. He was keen for Russia to accept the ideas of the West and at one time he forced the noblemen to shave off their beards. He founded the city of St Petersburg as his "window on the West".

REVOLUTION!

The last tsar of Russia was Nicholas II. He was a shy, kindly man with little interest in politics. He was unwise in his choice of ministers and his government was corrupt. People who opposed him were brutally dealt with by the secret police. There was deep unrest among ordinary people, who wanted more control over the government. In 1905 the tide of revolution which had swept the country was brought to an end when the tsar's bodyguards fired on the people of St Petersburg.

During World War 1 the government organized the war badly and Russia suffered disastrous defeats by Germany. There were mutinies and mass desertions by troops, and order broke down in the towns. Food was scarce, the transport system failed, and factories became desperately short of materials. Nicholas, who had taken command of the army, was prevented from returning to Moscow. In 1917 he was forced to abdicate.

Workers' councils soon took control of factories, and peasants began to seize land in the countryside. Popular support grew for Lenin and the revolutionaries. In November 1917 the revolutionary Bolshevik party, led by Vladimir Ilyich Lenin, seized power.

The "Mad Monk"
Grigori Rasputin was a Russian priest and faith healer. His ability to help Tsar Nicholas II's son Alexis, who suffered from the blood disease haemophilia, gave Rasputin power in the royal household. He was infamous for his drunken and shocking behaviour and his hypnotic power over people. Rasputin's friendship with the royal family made them even more unpopular with the people. In 1916, with the tsar occupied by the war, Rasputin was almost in charge of the country. He was finally murdered by a group of noblemen. First they tried to poison him, then they shot him, and in the end they had to drown him in the River Neva.

The last tsar
Nicholas II was the first cousin of George V of Britain. After abdicating in 1917, Nicholas was held prisoner by the secret police. The following year he, his wife and five children were shot and killed in the basement of a house in Western Siberia, where they were being held.

Father of Soviet Communism
Vladimir Ilyich Lenin joined the revolution after his elder brother was hanged for plotting to murder Tsar Alexander III. Lenin was imprisoned and then exiled for his revolutionary ideas. For some time he lived in London. In 1917 he returned to lead the Bolsheviks in the revolution. After Lenin's death in 1924 his body was embalmed and placed in a glass case in a mausoleum in Red Square. In this photograph, Lenin makes a speech to the troops in Moscow, in 1920.

Prophet of Communism
Karl Marx was a German philosopher whose book *Das Kapital* influenced Lenin and the Bolsheviks. Marx imagined a society with no class divisions. Everyone would be equal. There would be no private ownership and no government since the society would run itself on the principle, "From each according to his ability, to each according to his need".

THE UNION AT WAR

Lenin's successor as leader of the USSR was Joseph Stalin, a ruthless and ambitious man. He designed a series of Five-Year Plans to build up Soviet industry. The 1930s were years of desperate hardship for the people. Industrial expansion was pursued at any cost, and paid for by exporting farm produce to other countries. Food became scarce and starvation killed millions of people. Those who opposed Stalin were shot or sent to prison camps in Siberia.

The cost was high, but Stalin achieved his aim. Within 10 years Soviet industry was modern and strong. The country was ready to face the growing threat of Nazi Germany, led by Hitler, who was determined to crush Soviet communism.

World War 2 began. The Germans invaded the USSR in June 1941 and made rapid advances. Soviet troops fought desperately to keep the Germans at bay. The turning point of the war was the Battle of Stalingrad. The city was defended street by street in a bitter struggle. Eventually the Germans were forced to surrender. The Soviets, though victorious, lost a devastating 20 million people in the war.

Besieged!
The German siege of Leningrad lasted 879 days. The only means of supplying the city with food and medicines was across the frozen surface of Lake Ladoga, the "Road of Life". Here German shells explode in the city's streets.

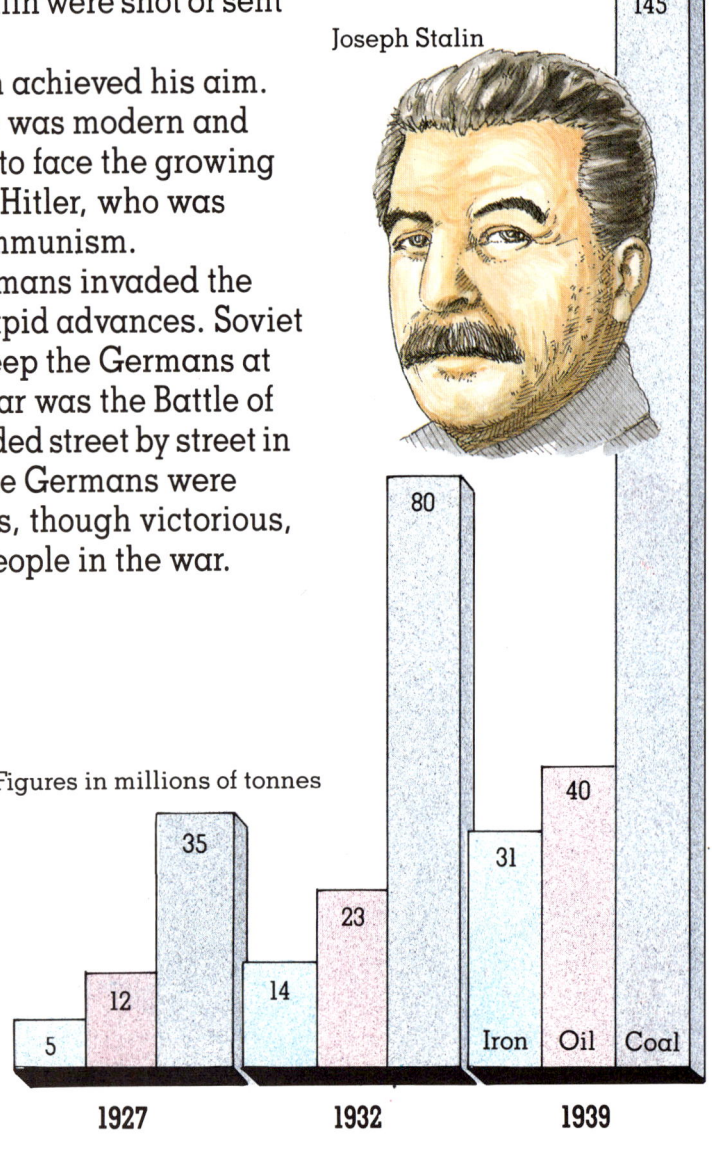

Joseph Stalin

Famine and starvation
There were several famines in the USSR in the years between World Wars 1 and 2. Millions of ordinary people died, despite food and money being sent from abroad. All the nation's effort was being put into strengthening industry and the armed forces. Stalin's plans worked, however, as you can see from these graphs of industrial output for the years between the two world wars.

Figures in millions of tonnes

The Iron Curtain falls

During World War 2 Joseph Stalin, the British Prime Minister Winston Churchill, and the American President Franklin D Roosevelt met to plan battles against the Nazis. But although these countries were united in war against the Nazis, there was suspicion between the USSR and the West in times of peace. After World War 2 the USSR and its allies withdrew behind the "Iron Curtain".

KEY FACTS

▶ 1922 The old Russian Empire becomes the Union of Soviet Socialist Republics (USSR).
▶ 1924 Lenin dies and Stalin becomes Soviet leader.
▶ 1929 Collectivization begins. The land is pooled into large units and farmed as "co-operatives".
▶ 1933 The Great Famine kills millions.
▶ 1941 Operation Barbarossa begins – the German invasion of the USSR.
▶ 1942 The long and terrible Battle of Stalingrad is at last won by the Soviets.
▶ 1945 The Iron Curtain falls across Europe.
▶ 1953 Stalin dies and Khrushchev becomes Soviet leader.

COMRADES IN COMMUNISM

The Communist Party is the only political party in the Soviet Union. The most powerful person in the party is the General Secretary, and the most important decision-making body is the Politburo. Only one citizen in 12 is a Communist Party member. Membership involves a lot of time and energy, and like people in many other countries, most ordinary Soviet citizens are not active in politics.

It is essential to be a party member for some important posts in the Civil Service and armed forces, and for some teaching jobs. The *Komsomol* is for young communists aged between 14 and 26 years.

The Communist Party has strict control over all aspects of Soviet life, including the news and programmes on television and radio, and what is published in newspapers and books. It is difficult for people to criticize the state openly. Those who complain about lack of freedom are called "dissidents" and are sometimes imprisoned.

The Soviet system
The word *soviet* means "council". Soviets form the basis of government in the USSR. They range from the small village soviet which controls local village affairs to the Supreme Soviet which is the USSR's "parliament". Only Communist Party members may stand for election to the soviets. So people can vote, but only for one party.

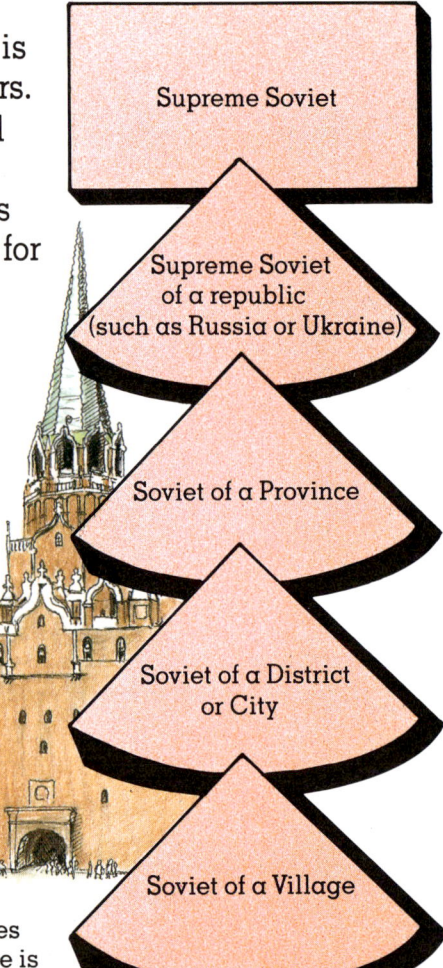

- Supreme Soviet
- Supreme Soviet of a republic (such as Russia or Ukraine)
- Soviet of a Province
- Soviet of a District or City
- Soviet of a Village

The Palace of Congress
This is part of the Kremlin (government headquarters) in Moscow. The Communist Party meets here to review policies and make plans. The palace is also used as a theatre.

The "Eastern Bloc"

This name is given to the group of countries in Eastern Europe which have communist governments. As in the USSR, the state controls many aspects of life in these countries, and the governments look to Moscow for guidance. These countries are shown in red on the map. The "motherland" (the USSR) is shown in pink.

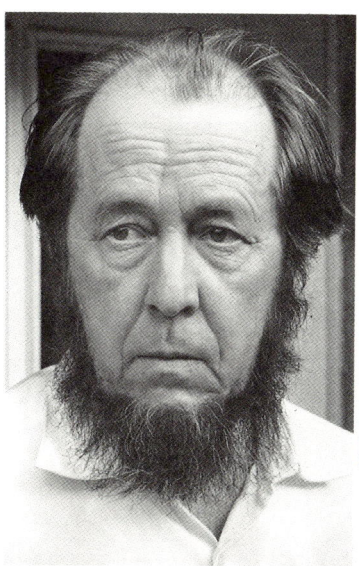

Writing in public

Alexander Solzhenitsyn is the most famous of present-day Soviet writers. He was expelled from the USSR in 1974 for condemning the policies of the government. His book *One Day in the Life of Ivan Denisovich* describes life in a Soviet prison camp. Despite being awarded the Nobel Prize for Literature in 1970, his books are not published in the Soviet Union. He now lives in the USA.

The power of the state

The Communist Party watches over many details of everyday life. A private letter posted from one person to another can be opened and read by the state censors. If the letter is critical of the government, then the writer may be in trouble.

RELIGION AND THE STATE

Russia officially adopted the Christian religion in the 10th century. The religious ideas came from the Greek branch of the Byzantine church based in Byzantium.

As the Russian Orthodox Church grew, it developed its own written language and religious art, in the form of elegant statues and ornate paintings. Beautiful churches with "onion"-shaped domes, many covered in sheet gold, were built all over the land. There were 400 churches in Moscow alone. The priests were firm supporters of the Russian tsars.

After the Revolution of 1917, the position of the church suddenly changed. Today the USSR is officially an atheist (non-believing) state. Religious worship is discouraged, and church congregations are usually made up of a few elderly people. Some religious groups, such as the Jews, have particular difficulties. Many Jews apply to leave the Soviet Union, to go to Israel.

One religious group which the Soviet government cannot ignore is the Muslim group. The traditional way of life in the Asiatic republics is firmly based in the Muslim religion and is not likely to give way to state atheism.

"A Happy New Year!"

С НОВЫМ ГОДОМ!

"Grandfather Frost"
In the USSR, old religious festivals such as Christmas and Easter have given way to modern non-religious versions. New Year is celebrated with the figure of Grandfather Frost, who brings presents and who looks remarkably like Santa Claus!

Golden domes
Many churches and cathedrals in the Soviet Union (like these in the Kremlin) are prized as architectural works of art. They are carefully restored, with real gold leaf on the domes. Yet their importance as religious buildings is overlooked.

Marriage, Moscow style
Today, weddings are civil and legal occasions rather than religious ceremonies. Couples marry in ornate offices called "palaces". Afterwards they may go to pay their respects at the local war memorial, as shown here.

ART AND ARCHITECTURE

In the past, Russian art was mainly religious. Churches were lavishly decorated inside, often with many beautiful painted ikons (religious portraits). The church buildings were modelled on the domed churches of Byzantium. They are still a common sight among modern city office blocks.

The houses of the past were usually simply made from natural materials such as wood. This tradition has largely given way to modern concrete construction. Low-rise apartment blocks are the most typical form of housing today.

Since the Revolution of 1917, Russian art has been used to celebrate the achievements of communism. The official view is that art should be realistic and should point the way forward. Any works that are critical of the state are strongly discouraged, and the artist may be punished.

KEY FACTS

▶ The Hermitage Museum (see below) contains two and a half million masterpieces of art, many by European artists.
▶ The Tretyakov Gallery in Moscow is devoted to a collection of Russian art. It contains 50,000 paintings and sculptures.
▶ Showing violence in works of art is seen as harmful to society and is discouraged by the State.

An open-air museum
The 22-domed church in Khizi, near Lake Baikal, was built in 1714 entirely of wood. No nails were used at all. Legend has it that when the architect, Nestor, completed the building he threw his axe into a lake, saying that there would never be anything like it again. Khizi is now an open-air museum. Other traditional wooden buildings have been moved there and re-erected as examples of old-style Russian craftsmanship.

Heroes of Stalingrad
These enormous statues were sculpted in memory of those who lost their lives in the Battle of Stalingrad, in World War 2. They are good examples of 20th century Soviet art. The style, "Socialist Realism", is intended to portray ordinary life and celebrate the values of Soviet socialism. Stalingrad has since been renamed Volgograd.

The Winter Palace
Tsar Peter the Great rejected Russian traditional architecture when he designed St Petersburg (now Leningrad), which is much more European-looking than other Soviet cities. His Winter Palace is now called the Hermitage and contains a world-famous collection of art.

MASTERS IN WORDS AND MUSIC

Visitors to the USSR usually find the Soviet people to be hospitable and generous, proud of their culture and fond of singing and dancing. The Soviets have a strong tradition of story-telling. This comes from the days when peasants gathered round the fire during the long winter to tell tales of witches, wolves, fairies and princesses. There is still a deep interest in folk art and stories today.

From these traditions come many world-famous novelists, such as Fyodor Dostoevsky, who wrote *Crime and Punishment* and *The Brothers Karamazov*. Anton Chekhov's plays and stories, such as *The Cherry Orchard*, also enjoy international fame.

In the 18th century the Russian nobles took an interest in ballet, under French influence. Pepita, Fokine and other creators of dance movements made great contributions to ballet. Many people regard Soviet dancers as the best in the world.

Some of the great Russian composers wrote music for the ballet, including Peter Tchaikovsky and Sergei Prokofiev. The composer Dmitry Shostakovich is famous for his *Leningrad Symphony*, which is dedicated to the victims of the 879-day Leningrad Siege in World War 2.

The composer supreme
Peter Ilyich Tchaikovsky (1840-1893) originally studied law and did not begin to write music until the age of 23. He made little money from his works for many years. Then, when he was 37, a wealthy music-lover, Nadeja von Meck, offered to support him – on the condition that they should never meet. They never did, although they exchanged letters. Tchaikovsky wrote six symphonies as well as music for ballets, of which *Swan Lake* and *The Nutcracker Suite* are the most famous.

From count to peasant
Count Leo Nikolaievich Tolstoy (1828-1919) is one of the greatest of all novelists. He was born on the family estate at Tula, which is about 100 miles south of Moscow. His epic novel *War and Peace* is set at the time when Napoleon invaded Russia in 1812. In later life Tolstoy gave up his property and wealth in order to live the life of an ordinary peasant.

Anna Pavlova

Vaslav Nijinsky

Rudolph Nureyev

Natalia Bessmertnova

A night at the ballet
The Bolshoi Ballet in Moscow and the Kirov Ballet in Leningrad have staged performances since the 18th century. They are amongst the most talented and well-rehearsed companies in the world. Their dancers have included Pavlova, Nijinsky and Nureyev.

A day at the circus
The Moscow State Circus is admired for the breathtaking performances of people and animals. The performing bears are especially famous.

SCHOOL DAYS

Education is seen as very important in the Soviet Union. Much time and money is put into teaching the future citizens of the country, and all children from the age of seven must go to school. Since many mothers have jobs, nurseries creches and kindergartens are provided to look after young children.

Most schools have a uniform – brown dresses for girls and grey suits for boys. On special days, such as 1 September when the school year starts, girls wear frilly white aprons and bows in their hair, and take bunches of flowers for the teacher.

The school day lasts from half past eight until about half past one. Older children spend the afternoons doing sports or private study in the classroom. Children of mixed abilities work together in the class. Most schools teach English from the age of 11.

There are a number of special schools in the USSR that concentrate on particular subjects. Children gifted in languages, music, ballet, art, maths or sport might go to one of these.

The daily diary
Each Soviet pupil has a school diary in which he or she writes homework. The teacher marks it out of 5:
- 5 – excellent
- 4 – good
- 3 – satisfactory
- 2 – poor
- 1 – fail

The parents sign the book after the teacher has filled it in. This way, parents always know how their children are doing at school!

Science City!
After secondary school, many pupils go on to further education in universities and institutes. This whole town, Akademgorok in Siberia, was built for educating and training young scientists and mathematicians.

Always ready

From the age of 10, children are encouraged to join the Pioneers, a national youth organization similar to the British Scouts or Guides. Pioneers make a promise to love their country and they wear a red neckchief and a badge which says "Always ready". (This is very similar to the Scout motto of "Be prepared".)

Pioneer Palaces

Out-of-school activities are held in Pioneer Palaces, which are old buildings converted into club houses for the Pioneers. There are all sorts of activities including music, athletics, nature study and electronics. Pioneers can also go on holiday to summer camp. The most famous camp is at Artek, on the Black Sea (shown here).

LOOKING AFTER THE PEOPLE

For centuries the Russians, like many other peoples, relied on folk medicine and natural remedies to cure illness. Many of their treatments came from the East, brought by the Mongol invaders of the 13th century. Cures were administered by the *Znakhari*, the "knowledgeable people" who kept their secrets in the family, passing them from one generation to the next. Today, folk medicine is still used, respected and encouraged by doctors in many parts of the Soviet Union.

The 20th century, however, has seen many advances in scientific medicine. There is now less illness, and people live longer. Good medical care is free to all Soviet citizens.

Part of the reason for Soviet healthiness is the importance of exercise and sport in schools, factories and offices. The USSR is among the world leaders in many sports, including ice hockey, ice skating, basketball, weightlifting, gymnastics, and athletic events of all kinds.

Soviet weightlifters lead the world

Valeriy Borzov
Soviet sprinter, winner of 100 and 200 metres Olympic gold medals (1972)

Olga Korbut
Soviet gymnast, winner of four Olympic gold medals (1972 and 1976)

It's a record!
The scoresheets of the World Championships and Olympic Games are full of Soviet names and records. The USSR women's gymnastics team has won the Olympic gold medal a record eight times. Nikolai Andrianov won 15 Olympic gold medals between 1972 and 1980 – a record for a male gymnast. The Soviets dominate the "power" field sports such as throwing the shot, discus and javelin.

Mud cures

Health-cure houses and rest homes are common in the Black Sea resorts. Factories often send their workers there, partly as a holiday and partly for treatment for illness. Covering the body in warm mud is a traditional treatment for rheumatism and arthritis.

Elixir of youth

The people of the Caucasian mountains, near the Black Sea, are famous for their long life. Many live to be over 100 years old. Here Khanlar Guseinov (125 years old), from near Lachin, chats to his great-great-grandson while working on the farm. The following ancient recipe is said to prolong youth:

Mix 1 lb garlic, finely ground, with the juice of 24 lemons. Leave for 24 days. Take a teaspoon each night.

VANYA'S DAY

Vanya is 15 and lives with his parents, in a flat on the outskirts of Moscow. The family is fortunate in having two bedrooms, so Vanya can have a room of his own. He gets up at seven o'clock, ready for school at half past eight. His mother makes fried eggs, bread and butter and tea for breakfast. Vanya takes some money to buy a bun at morning break. Both his parents work, so he has his lunch at school.

School finishes at half past two. Today is Wednesday, so Vanya will spend the afternoon at the geological society meeting in the local Pioneer Palace (see page 37).

Vanya's parents come home at about five o'clock, although his mother is sometimes late if she has to queue for food at the local stores. When she gets in she prepares a meal, perhaps *kotleki*, a kind of beefburger with salad. There might even be ice-cream in the fridge! At nine o'clock the family watches *Vremya*, the main TV news.

At the weekend they might visit a cinema or museum. Vanya is looking forward to Sunday, when he'll be going with his father to watch football at the Lenin Stadium.

Living in the city
The standard of living is gradually increasing for many Soviet families:
▶ Most Soviet people live in small flats. There are about two and a half million flats in Moscow alone.
▶ In most households both parents go to work, but mothers still do most of the housework!
▶ The usual day off is Sunday. People generally spend it doing sporting activities or leisure pursuits such as fishing.
▶ Consumer goods are becoming more widely available. There are now 102 televisions for every 100 families in the USSR.

Summer home from home
A few families own a *dacha* or summer cottage where they can spend weekends and holidays. These are often traditional wooden buildings on the outskirts of towns, where people can relax and enjoy country pastimes like mushrooming in the woods.

Queuing for a treat

A Soviet foodstore is called a *Gastronom* and sells most kinds of foods, except fruit and vegetables. Supplies can be irregular, and customers may spend a long time queuing for something special. It may be necessary to queue three times: once to ask for the goods, then again to pay, and again to collect the parcel!

Flat life

By British standards, a typical Soviet flat is quite small – perhaps two rooms with a kitchen and bathroom. Many families have a bed in the living room. Rents are low and usually include the central heating, which is switched on from 1 October to 1 May – whatever the weather!

CABBAGE SOUP AND VODKA

In the USSR, traditional food varies across the country according to the climate and the main crops. In the south, where it is warm, fruit is a main ingredient in the diet and also lamb, because of the many sheep grazed there. In the cold, wet lands of the north, cabbages, potatoes and fish are common foods. *Shchi*, a soup made from fresh cabbage, is very popular in these parts. The well-known dish called *borsht* comes from the central Soviet Union. It contains a mixture of vegetables, the chief one being beetroot (which gives it a rich red colour), sharpened with vinegar.

Under Tsar Peter the Great, Western styles of cooking reached the country. French chefs, employed by the nobility, invented such famous dishes as Chicken Kiev, Beef Stroganoff and Charlotte Russe.

Traditional drinks include *kvass*, a kind of weak beer which is often sold on the street, and *koumiss*, a speciality of the central Asian republics, made from fermented mare's milk.

Today, ice-cream is very popular in the Soviet Union. In every town there are ice-cream parlours with names like "Polar Bear" or "Blizzard". Even in the depths of winter, people can be seen in the streets licking an ice-cream.

Anyone for tea?
The Soviets are great tea drinkers. The *samovar*, heated by charcoal, is the traditional way of making tea and is often very ornate. A small pot of strong tea is kept warming on top of the *samovar* and water is used to dilute it. Men usually take their tea in glasses and women have it in china cups. Tea is mostly drunk with lemon and sugar, although in country districts a spoonful of jam is sometimes used to sweeten it.

A mouth-watering selection of zakuski

A little of what you fancy

Zakuski is the name given to Russian hors d'oeuvres or starters. It consists of titbits to tempt the appetite and may include caviar, paté, smoked sausage, salted herring, dill, potatoes and cucumber. Sometimes foreign guests mistake the lavish *zakuski* for the main meal, and they eat so much that they have no room left for the dinner that follows!

Pelmeni

Famous dishes from the USSR

Shashlik A Caucasian dish of lamb cooked on a spit over charcoal, like a kebab.
Kasha A kind of porridge made of cereals, usually buckwheat.
Tvorozhniki A cheese pancake often served with *smetana* (soured cream).
Pelmeni A Siberian dish, like ravioli, filled with meat or fish.
Kissil Fruit jelly.

Cheers, comrade!

Vodka is a drink that is always associated with the USSR. It is distilled from grain and served at special meals and celebrations. It usually comes in a small glass and is meant to be drunk in a single gulp. Huge quantities of vodka are consumed at New Year.

Shaslik

Tvorozhniki

THE SOVIET UNION AND THE FUTURE

The year 1987 marked the 70th anniversary of the Communist Revolution in old Russia. Times of great hardship have given way to prosperity. The USSR is now one of the world's superpowers, rivalling the USA in military strength, industrial power and in the space race.

But the Soviet military and space programmes are expensive. They use up enormous amounts of money which might be better spent elsewhere. Despite the progress of the last 70 years, farming is still not efficient enough to feed all the people. Wheat has to be imported from the West.

Soviet industry needs more investment, and the quality of many Soviet goods is poor. Young people are increasingly demanding Western-style consumer goods like jeans and pop records.

Politically, the nation has not reached the ultimate goal of communism as prophesied by Karl Marx, where all class divisions disappear. The Soviet citizen lacks freedom in speech and writing. However, in the 1980s the country's leadership began to tackle some of these problems and showed signs of wishing to raise the Iron Curtain between East and West.

A new policy?
Under Mikhail Gorbachev, leader of the USSR since 1985, the nation pursued a policy known as *glasnost* – "openness". The aim was to reduce the restrictions on the lives of ordinary Soviet people and have freer communications with the rest of the world.

Nuclear arms treaty
Both the USSR and the USA have enough nuclear weapons to destroy each other many times over. Meetings are held regularly between the two countries, mostly in Geneva, in Switzerland, to try and reach agreement in reducing the numbers of nuclear missiles. Here the President of the USA, Ronald Reagan, meets USSR leader, Mikhail Gorbachev.

Superpower in space
The USSR spends billions of roubles on its space programmes. It launched the first satellite into space, *Sputnik*, in 1961. The Soviet cosmonaut Yuri Gagarin (above) was the first person in space, in 1963. The USSR plans to launch its own version of the Space Shuttle, and to build a permanently manned space station, *Mir*.

Index

Akademgorok 36
Alexander II 22
Alexander III 25
architecture 32, 33
art 32
Artek 37
ballet 34, 35
Black Sea 10, 11, 37
Bolshevik Party 24, 25
Byelorussia 20, 21
Catherine the Great 22
caviar 12
Chernobyl 18
churches 30, 31, 32, 33
circus 35
climate 10, 11
clothing 10, 11, 18, 20, 21
collectives 17, 18, 27
Communist Party 6, 28, 29
composers 34
currency 7
Cyrillic alphabet 8
desert 10, 11, 12, 13
Eastern Bloc 29
education 36, 40
employment 19
energy 18, 19
family life 40
farming 16, 17, 18, 27, 42, 44
fishing 13
folklore and customs 20, 21, 34
food 40, 41, 42, 43
Gagarin, Yuri 44
gemstones 17, 18
Georgia 11, 16, 21
Gorbachev, Mikhail 44
history 22, 23, 24, 25, 26, 27, 30
housing 32, 41
industry 18, 19, 26, 44
Iron Curtain 27
Ivan the Terrible 22
Karakum desert 10, 11
Khizi 33
Kiev 7
Kremlin 28, 31
Lake Baikal 12, 13
language 8, 9
Lenin, Vladimir Ilyich 24, 25, 27

Leningrad 7, 10, 26, 33, 34, 35
Marx, Karl 24, 25, 44
medicine 38, 39
minerals 16, 17, 18
Moscow 6, 7, 15, 19, 25, 28, 29, 32, 35, 40
Nicholas II 24
nuclear power 18
oil 17, 18, 19
Omayakon Valley 10
Palace of Congress 28
peoples 20, 21
Peter the Great 7, 22, 23, 33, 42
Pioneers 37, 40
politics 28, 29, 44
population 7
Pravda 9
Rasputin, Grigori 24
religion 30, 31
republics 6, 7, 20, 28
revolution 24, 25, 30, 32, 44
Romanov family 22
Russian language 8, 9
Russian republic 6, 7
St Basil's Cathedral 6, 22
St Cyril 8

St Petersburg 7, 22, 23, 33
Samarkand 21
Siberia 6, 10, 16, 18, 36
Solzhenitsyn, Alexander 29
soviets 28
space programme 44, 45
sport 38
Stalin, Joseph 26, 27
Stalingrad 26, 27, 33
steppe 12, 13
taiga 12, 13
Tallin 7, 41
TASS 8
Tchaikovsky, Peter Ilyich 34
timber industry 16, 18, 19
Tolstoy, Leo Nikolaievich 34
transport 14, 15
Trans-Siberian Railway 14, 15
tsar 22, 23, 24
tundra 12, 13
Ukraine 7, 16, 17
vodka 43
Volograd 33
wildlife 12, 13
World Wars 24, 26, 27, 33, 34
writers 29, 34

Acknowledgements
All illustrations by Ann Savage.
Photographic credits (a = above, b = below, m = middle, l = left, r = right):
Cover *al* E&P Bauer/Zefa, *bl* Goebel/Zefa, *ar* A Marakov/Novosti Press Agency, *br* Y Kuidin/Novosti Press Agency; page 9 Barry Lewis/Network; page 11 Intourist; page 13 Novosti Press Agency; page 14 Intourist; page 15 P Nugent; page 17 Y Kuidin/Novosti Press Agency; page 18 Novosti Press Agency; page 19 Barry Lewis/Network; pages 20 and 21 G Medvedev/Novosti Press Agency; page 22 BPCC/Aldus Archive; page 23 I Nikitin/Novosti Press Agency; pages 24 and 25 Novosti Press Agency; page 27 B Kudoyarov/Novosti Press Agency; page 29 UPI/Bettman Archive/BBC Hulton Picture Library; page 31 *a* Damn/Zefa, *b* Zefa; page 33 Novosti Press Agency; page 35 Robert Harding Associates; page 36 John Massey Stewart; page 37 *a* and *b* Novosti Press Agency; page 39 *a* Andrzej Jaroszewicz, *b* Y Rakhil/Novosti Press Agency; page 42 Intourist; page 44 *a* Nex, *b* Novosti Press Agency; page 45 *a* Novosti Press Agency/Science Photo Library, *b* Novosti Press Agency.